Train Ride *Through* Heaven

DAVIDA COLEMAN

Ordering Information:

Prime Seven Media
518 Landmann St.
Tomah City, WI 54660

Printed in the United States of America

A Train Ride Through Heaven

Put your seatbelts on, strap yourself in and get
ready for a magical ride and time of your life!

As this set of train tracks are headed directly
for Heaven, and the people who live there.

It Cost Nothing to Activate Your Imagination....,

The good news is, no fee is required, all you need now to get this train moving is...., one healthy imagination to reach your destination!

Now that this train is in motion, do not lose
your train of thought, as it will be your guide
that secures your ride and not go a float.

Entering God's Country
Who's Waiting For Us

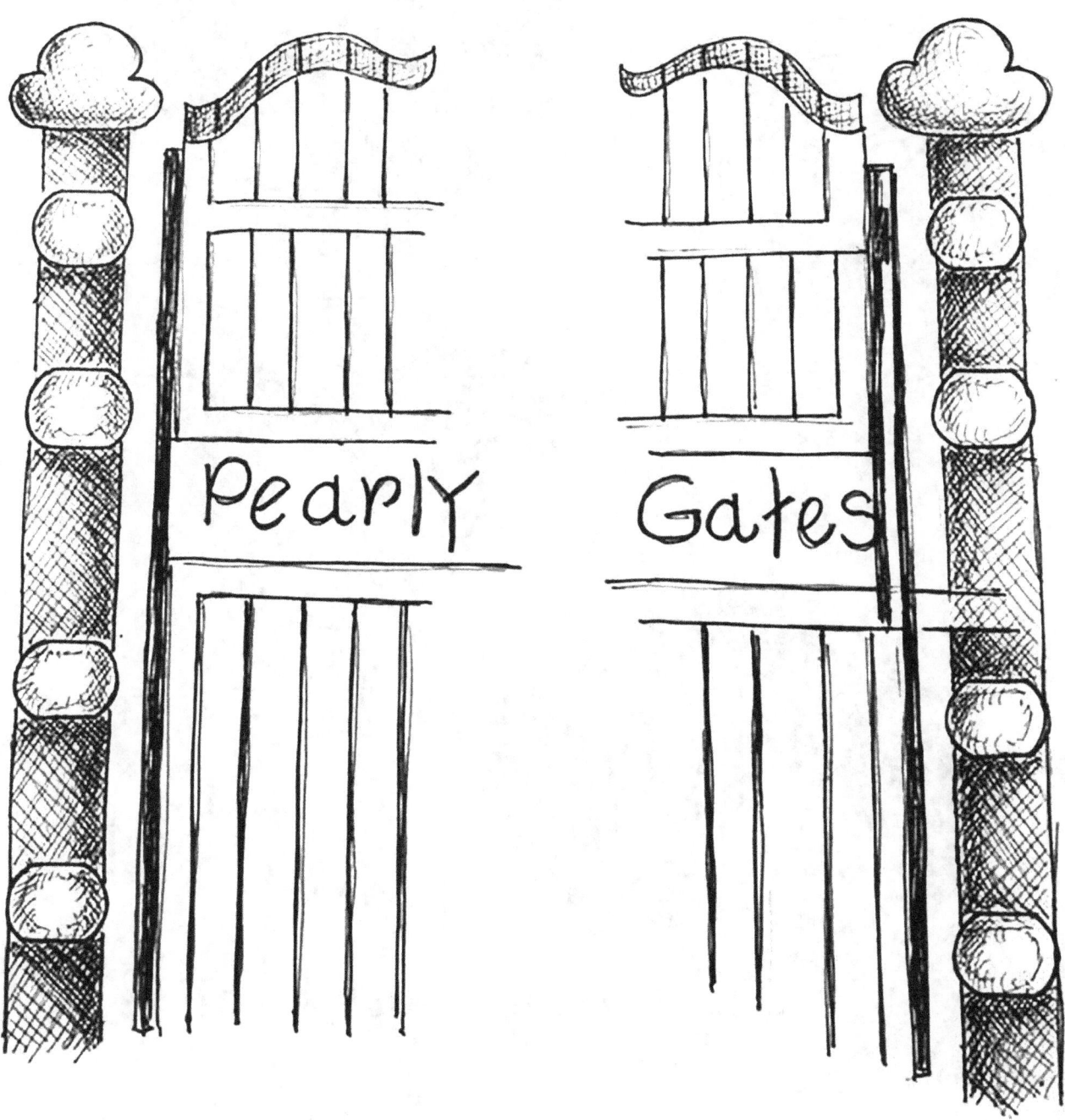

So hold on tight, as we have now reached our
destination, the Pearly Gates are opening
and let's see who we have waiting.

Hedven looks
different for edch
of Us ...

Now here's the point where for some of us
Heaven may start to look a little different.

The train is now pulling into the station. Some of
us will begin to see our loved ones greet us.

The Angels look down From Heaven to see who they must greet, as some of us have not yet experienced Loss

For some of you who have not yet experienced loss,
it will be the Angels there that will greet you

But for those of us who have, we can't even begin to imagine where to look, to find our moms and dads.

"Oh", there they are, look! Standing just beyond
the platform at the station, waving to us and
on the right of them is our old neighbors.

After seeing all of our loved ones and
visiting with them, it's now time to go.

Not a minute to spare, as our fuel is now running low, and we begin to float- as our imagination is now about to move onto its next destination.... Home sweet home we go.

We all begin to waive goodbye, as we once
again step aboard to make our journey
back home, to Heaven on Earth.

As we return- we do not carry with us a care or concern.
We arrive back home with a smile on our faces- knowing
our loved ones are with God, and very much well cared for.

As our train ride was that of an express one, so is our return
ticket back home, so is our purpose. To explain to the world
that there is no room for or of sadness in God's house
where all of our loved ones go when they go home to God.

There are only rooms filled with joy as he
and the angels created it that way.

Heaven's Gate

So, if here on earth you feel a little down or sad, no need for worries, you too can do the same as us kids. By using your free ticket, hopping aboard the express train and taking a ride through Heaven to visit your loved ones no matter who that might be.

Again, just like us kids the same is true for you. I know someone up there is waiting to say hello to you.

Remember, all you need to get your train in motion
is a little imagination! So enjoy the ride, enjoy the
scenes and remember, you can always Dream.

NOW ALL ABOARD BEFORE THE NEXT TRAIN LEAVES

THE END